# An Educational Organizational Puzzle:

# Professional Learning Communities With Fidelity

## Dr. Natasha Cox-Magno

# PERSPECTIVES

Your strategic book title, *An Educational Organizational Puzzle: Professional Learning Communities with Fidelity* captured my attention.

Effective professional learning communities are needed now to instructionally support the academic and socio-emotional needs of the whole child.

The time is now!

It is a must read for educators!

Todd Feltman, PhD
Author of *Transforming Into Powerful Third, Fourth, or Fifth Grade Navigators of School Success*

-----------------------------------------------------------------------

It is a very complete work and I believe strongly in the community concept. Thank you for this opportunity. Good job!

Curt Richards
Author of *30 Insights for New Teachers to Thrive*

-----------------------------------------------------------------------

Drawing from my background in ongoing educational enhancement, I am confident this will steer educators and administrators toward a more holistic planning approach, fostering an alternative perspective and innovative mindset.

Andrew McGee
Author of *Champion and Champion Forever*

As an educational leader who has experienced firsthand the transformative impact of Professional Learning Communities (PLCs), I am thrilled to endorse *An Educational Organizational Puzzle: Professional Learning Communities With Fidelity*. This book offers an exceptional foundation on the fundamental concepts of PLCs, making it an indispensable resource for educators at any level of their career. Whether you are just beginning to explore the potential of PLCs or looking to deepen your existing knowledge, this text serves as an ideal entry point.

Dr. Cox-Magno has masterfully outlined the key principles that make PLCs effective, including collaborative learning, shared leadership, and continuous improvement. Her practical approach, backed by solid research, provides readers with the tools necessary to implement PLCs in ways that can significantly enhance the educational experience and outcomes within their schools.

I highly recommend this book to all educators who are committed to fostering a culture of collaboration and sustained academic excellence. Dive into this text, and you'll find invaluable insights that will help you and your team unlock the full potential of your learning community.

Charles Williams
Founder of CW Consulting Educational Services

# ACKNOWLEDGEMENTS

**I would like to thank……**

My parents Alejandro Cox and Rosella Cox for providing a family environment that incorporated a family learning community by sitting around the dinner table every night to discuss our day, solve problems and plan future family events.

My husband, Dave Magno, supported me by looking at problems to obtain successful solutions for my students' continuous educational improvement. He is a great thinker and listener.

Dr. Peter Ross (Doctoral Chairperson) who continues to support me throughout my life's journey for success with sincerity.

My first educational leader, Ms. Orlando. She provided a professional learning community that supported building my real-world experience educational knowledge capacity as well as sustainability.

Dr. Todd Feltman, for his continuous and generous support. A colleague and friend with an overwhelming-welcoming gracious personality.

Curt Richards and Andrew McGee for taking time out of their day to review and provide valuable insight for this book.

# MEET THE AUTHOR

Dr. Natasha Cox-Magno is interested in how to improve scholars' educational experience. Her first book "A Purposeful Reading Journey With a Metacognitive Approach" focused on using a purpose to increase focus, engagement, and comprehension.

However, there is more to supporting scholars in a multi structured educational system. This book provides a focus based approach on improving educational environments as well as supporting educators, parents, and administrators' collaborative efforts for scholars' educational success.

Dr. Natasha Cox- Magno's credentials and experience supports her knowledge pertaining to professional learning communities. She is a peer-reviewed author, a researcher, and an educator. Also, Dr. Cox-Magno founded a nonprofit educational enrichment organization,"Accentuating Learning Inc.".

Dr. Natasha Cox-Magno earned a B.A in Psychology and a Master's of Science in Education, as well as degrees as a School Administrator and Supervision, and School District Administrator. She also obtained a Doctorate in Education that incorporated research, administration, and educational instructional studies. Dr. Cox-Magno has been involved in professional learning communities through research, participation, and assisting in developing professional learning communities.

Dr. Natasha Cox-Magno has noted that she loves professional communities because it gives everyone a voice through collaborative efforts to support scholars by building successful educational capacity and sustainability. She can be found at "My Reading *Nook*" site, *LinkedIn*, and *Instagram*.

Dr. Natasha Cox-Magno is open to book talks and book signings.

**My Reading Nook**

# TABLE OF CONTENTS

# FIDELITY

Traditionally, "implemented with fidelity" has been defined as the degree of adherence to an instructional plan (Cook & Smith, 2012; Harn, Parisi & Stoolmiller, 2013; Kutash, Cross, Madias, Duchnowski, & Green, 2012).

Currently, the definition of"implemented with fidelity"has been extended to not only treatment exposure, treatment quality or competence, but also program differentiation, participant exposure, and participant responsiveness (Cook & Smith, 2012;. Harn, Parisi & Stoolmiller, 2013; Kutash et al., 2012).

## Southwest Educational Development Laboratory (SEDL)

SEDL (2024) conveyed, "SEDL's mission was to strengthen the connection among research, policy, and practice in order to improve outcomes of all learners" (p 1).

# INTRODUCTION

Dear Educators, Administrators, Future Educators, and Families,

Schools are institutional educational systems that have many interrelated levels. These educational instructional systems are responsible for educating many scholars with many different types of personalities, educational and social emotional needs. Moreover, it takes many people to come together, collaborate, apply, intertwine their ideas to develop and sustain an effective learning community in a professional way.

This guide provides suggested ideas related to professional learning communities (PLC). You will also see note sections for reflective purposes related to the read section. There is a PLC guided form to support fidelity implementation. Also, I provided PowerPoint slides with cumulative information related to PLC. You may use all of the suggested ideas, some of the key ideas, or adjust the key ideas to support your learning community.

With Intentions for Much Success

Dr. Natasha Cox-Magno

# IDEA ONE: THEORETICAL PERSPECTIVES

You may be wondering why I began this book with a theoretical lens. According to the American Museum of Natural History (2023), "A theory is a well-substantiated explanation of an aspect of the natural world that can incorporate laws, hypotheses and facts" (page 1). In other words, a theoretical perspective can provide a reason for essential professional learning community elements to be applied when developing a professional learning community.

In addition, you may be wondering why I aligned evidence-based research with the presented theories. The American Museum of Natural History (2023) discussed, "New evidence should be compatible with a theory"(page 1). Moreover, American Museum of Natural History (2023) stated, "The longer the central elements of a theory hold — the more observations it predicts, the more tests it passes, the more facts it explains — the stronger the theory"(page 1). In other words, the evidence based research supports how the theory is continuously conveyed and effectively proven in real world situations.

Therefore, applying relevant theories can support the development of professional learning community concepts into effective real world professional learning communities.

### Transformational Learning Theory

Jack Mezirow's perspective of transformational learning is based on educators making meaning in their lives and learning (McComish & Parson, 2013). Transformational learning is built on the belief that educators can improve their existing knowledge through discourse with other educators (Herlo, 2010). Thus, it is through collaborative efforts that educators learn from one another to improve students' learning.

In addition, transformational learning provides a supportive environment for educators (Mc Comish & Parson, 2013). The supportive environment occurs when educators are placed into teams for decision- making purposes.

Transformational learning is a process that transforms educators' perspective (Mc Comish & Parson, 2013). Furthermore, it is during the collaborative process that educators critically reflect on their knowledge, critically others knowledge and examine their reason for making a decision (Herlo, 2010). This transformational learning process consists of the following:

- Transforms a person's perspective of themselves.
- Transforms a person's belief system.
- Transforms a person's lifestyle.

Hence, these transformational process elements are a systematic way that educators come to a new perspective about how to implement and sustain effective instructional practices.

Mc Comish and Parsons (2010) discussed that Mezirow believed transformational learning derives from (a) extending an existing point of reference, (b) acquiring new points for reference, (c) changing perceptions, or (d) changing habits of the mind. For this reason, an educational system can either provide ways for educators to learn more about an existing effective educational practice, or can assist educators with ways to find new educational practices.

Also, the change in educators' perspectives can be a result of educators extending on existing knowledge or finding new effective educational practices. Nevertheless, extending knowledge about an existing practice or finding a new practice will involve collaboration among educators.

## Complexity Theory

Complexity theory is a phenomenon that is made up of independent and complex units (He, 2014). Thus, the educational system consists of the government, the school district, the school level, the teachers, the parents, and the students. These units are complex because they are made up of subunits (He, 2014).

The government provides educational rules and regulations. The school district consists of many schools and district leaders. The schools consist of school leaders, teachers, related service providers, parents and students. The people within the school system have different cultures and knowledge backgrounds. The various units within the phenomena interrelate with one another (He, 2014). The different people within the school system collaborate with one another. The units interrelate with one another to achieve a shared goal (He, 2014). The shared objective of the school system is to educate the students.

## Ethical Leadership Theory

Ethical leadership theory is based on three major components. The three main elements are an individual's intentions, choosing the correct method of doing good, and choosing the proper end (Wart, 2013). In other words, ethical leadership principles are based on an individual having good intentions to promote effective leadership for the common good. The qualities that leaders will need to implement ethical leadership are integrity, authenticity, empathy, and altruism (Wart, 2013). Therefore, ethical leaders will need to do the following:

- Be honest and trustworthy.
- Understand both their own perspective, and others' perspective for decision-making purposes.

- Be compassionate.
- Put the needs of the organization and the people in the organization first.

## *Dynamic Human-Centered Communication System Theory*

The dynamic human-centered communication system theory describes a communication style. Lang (2014) describes the dynamic human-centered communication system theory as a person in a specific location interacting over time with either another person or with a medium (i.e: in person, social media, emails, written letters or documents). Human-centered is described as all-important concepts and theoretical relationships start with human-constant elements (Lang, 2014). These constant human elements consist of interpersonal, mediated, group, or mass (Lang, 2014). The number of people increases, regarding the constant human element communication, in increments beginning at interpersonal to mass.

The system's dynamics consist of the following elements (Lang, 2014):

- The location of the person that starts the communication.
- The location of the communication partner or partners.
- The length of the interaction.
- The medium that carries the communication interactions.
- The content of the interactions.
- The partner(s) immersed in the interactions.

## *Adult Learning Theory*

Adult learning theory (or andragogy theory) is based on ways that adults learn. Bates (2016) stated, "Knowles argued that most adults want to be in control of their learning"(page 60). In other words, adult learning is intrinsically motivated.

In alignment with Bates (2016), Aguilar and Cohen (2022), provided the following components that are essential for adult learning:

- Adults must feel safe to learn.
- Adults come to learn experiences with histories.
- Adults need to learn why we have to learn something.
- Adults want agency in learning.
- Adults need practice to internalize learning.
- Adults have a problem centered approach to learning.
- Adults want to learn.

Thus, it can be determined that in order for adults to engage in a learning task, the above element must be in the context of their learning environment.

## Reflective Notes

Thinking about PLCs, which theory resonates with you the most?

_____

_____

_____

Provide an example of how the theory is applied in your PLCs?

_____

_____

_____

How would you apply a theory in your PLCs?

_____

_____

_____

# IDEA TWO: RESEARCH THAT SUPPORTS THEORIES

## Research that Supports Transformational Learning

### Harris and Jones (2010)

Transformational learning theory guides and supports professional learning communities. A Harris and Jones (2010) study discussed that professional learning community elements are aligned with the transformational learning theory.

Just like transformational learning theory, the professional learning community's purpose is to support students' learning by educators learning from each other through a collaboration process (Harris & Jones, 2010). The same study mentions that professional learning community characteristics consist of sharing information, learning from one another, collaboration, reflecting on practices, refining practices, collective responsibility, and shared leadership (Harris & Jones, 2010). Professional learning communities also should provide supportive environments for educators to collaborate (Harris & Jones, 2010).

Therefore, transformational learning guides professional learning communities by providing a supportive collaborative environment, sharing the same purpose, and sharing the same infrastructure characteristics.

## Research that Supports Complexity Theory

### Debnam, Pas, and Bradshaw (2012)

The school-wide positive behavioral intervention and support system is aligned with the complexity theory. Debnam, Pas, and Bradshaw (2012) discussed the school-wide positive behavioral intervention and support system. Just like the complexity theory, the school-wide behavioral support system is made of different units. These units are called the student support teams (Debnam et al., 2012).

Just like complexity theory, the school-wide positive behavioral intervention and support system has subunits. The subunits consist of the state, the school districts, the school, the administrators, the teachers, the health service providers and the students (Debnam et al., 2012).

The people within the school-wide positive behavioral intervention and support system collaborate with one another. The people on the student support team collaborate with one another to monitor the students' progress (Debnam et al., 2012).

Moreover, in order to have cohesive subunits for effective results, the school-wide positive behavioral intervention and the support system will need to have a common goal. That goal is to increase positive behaviors of students with social-emotional disabilities (Debnam et al., 2012). Therefore, the school-wide positive behavioral support system is aligned with complexity theory by using a system made up of multiple units that collaborate with one another for a common goal.

### Research that Supports Ethical Leadership

### Bouchamma's and Brie's (2014) Study

In Bouchamma's and Brie's 2014 study, they examined ethical leadership in professional communities of practice (CoP) in a school setting. This study used the six principles of school leaders' roles and responsibilities from Hord and Sommers' (2011) research study. The six principles were communication, collaboration, coaching, conflict resolution, change management, and support (Bouchamma and Brie, 2014).

Also, this research study used seven ethical leadership principles from the Kalshoven's et al. (2011) research study. The seven ethical leadership principles were justice, shared leadership, role clarification, solicitude, perspective, promoting ethical behavior, and integrity.

In the Bouchamma and Brie (2014) study, school leaders and teachers were interviewed about not only their experiences in CoP, but also their relationships with the members of the CoP. The results showed that communicator, coaching, collaborator, conflict resolution, and change agent were leadership roles associated with ethical leadership.

Ethical leadership theory supports Bouchamma and Brie's (2014) study. Just like ethical leadership, the Bouchamma and Brie (2014) study examined the same principles of ethical leadership. Just like the ethical leadership theory, the Bouchamma and Brie (2014) study proved that shared leadership and authentic collaboration is an important element in leading a school. The study proved that caring for the community and people in the community are important elements for leading a school.

Additionally, the Bouchamma and Brie's (2014) study proved that defining roles were important. Therefore, ethical leadership theory and Bouchamma and Brie (2014) are aligned because they identified the same ethical principles as being important for a school leader.

## Research that Supports Dynamic Human Centered Learning Theory

In Lee and Lang's 2015 study, they discussed the real-time combined impact of cognitive overload variables on available resources over the course of an hour-long television news program. This article defines cognitive overload as"redundancy, complexity, and emotion"(Lee and Lang 2015).

A qualitative methodology was applied by encoding the real-time combined impact of cognitive overload variables on available resources. According to Lee and Lang's (2015) study,"The results suggest that defining message variables in terms of dynamic changes in cognitive load can allow us to predict the simultaneous dynamic impact of multiple message variables which contribute to complexity on processing capacity and message processing"(page 599). In other words, how a person understands, stores, and receives a message is dependent on how the message is communicated.

### Research that Supports: Adult Learning Theory / Andragogy

In a 2014 study by Zepada, Parylo, and Bengtson, the researchers examined the current principal's administrative practices, and also explored the applied adult learning theory components throughout the principal's professional development sessions across four school systems in Georgia.

This study was conducted using a qualitative methodology. The results of this study indicated self-direction, problem-centered, motivated, relevancy-oriented and goal-oriented were the five adult learning theory components that were applied during a principal's professional development about current administrative practices over the four school systems. In addition, the results conveyed that the most essential current principal practices were situations aligned to daily work and barriers due to relevancy-oriented and problem-centered adult theory components reoccurring most frequently.

Adult Learning Theory supports Zepada, Parylo, and Bengtson's (2014) study. In alignment with the Adult Learning Theory, Zepada, Parylo and Bengtson's (2014) study identified the same elements related to adult learning. Just like Adult Learning Theory, Zepada, Parylo, and Bengtson's (2014) study showed that the Adult Learning theory components were present during professional development of current principal practices.

## Reflective Notes

Which study do you find most helpful for the development of your PLCs ?

_____

_____

_____

How would you apply your preferred study to develop your PLCs ?

_____

_____

_____

# IDEA THREE: POLICIES AND INFRASTRUCTURES

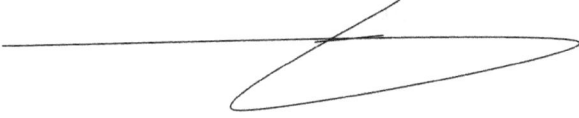

There are many policies that have been developed to guide educational practices. In 2001, the reauthorization of ESEA required states to (a) implement rigorous academic and achievement standards, (b) measure students' state assessment results to state standards, (c) be accountable for students' aggregated performance and students' disaggregated performance and (d) be held accountable for students meeting specific levels on assessments, attendance, and graduation rates (McLaughlin, Smith & Wilkinson, 2012).

Also, in 1997 IDEA required states to not only include students with disabilities in state exams, but also to report their exam scores (McLaughlin, Smith & Wilkinson, 2012). In addition, in 2004 IDEA required states to report the number of students with disabilities (a) taking the regular state exams without accommodations, (b) taking the state exams with accommodations, and (c) taking alternate state exams (McLaughlin, Smith & Wilkinson, 2012).

Furthermore, in June of 2010, 48 states agreed to implement the common core standards (McLaughlin, Smith & Wilkinson, 2012). As a result of the common core standards, the Council of Chief State School Education Officers (CCSSO) and the National Governors Association (NGA) recommended that the students with disabilities be provided with accommodations, assistive technology, and universal learning to support them with receiving rigorous academics (McLaughlin, Smith & Wilkinson, 2012). Even though the policies were put in place, there was still a need for an educational system to develop educational policies into effective educational practices.

Professional learning communities and professional infrastructures will assist educators in developing educational practices based on educational policies. Professional learning communities are an organizational system implemented to assist educators in increasing their knowledge to sustain students' learning performance using collaboration (The Center for Continuous Reform, 2009; Hargreaves & Fullan, 2012). Hence, the professional learning communities have professional infrastructure that support educators with becoming experts in their field to continuously increase their knowledge (experts) and to sustain effective educational practices.

The professional infrastructures are (a) effective educational policies that guide educational practices, (b) professional developments, (c) data driven instruction, (d) ample funding for programming, (e) adjusting intervention to meet the students' learning needs, (f) progress monitoring and (g) collaboration (Coleman, Gallagher, and Job, 2012 ;Hirsh & Hord, 2010; Buffum, Mattos, & Weber, 2012; Hargreaves & Fullan, 2012). Therefore, these professional infrastructures support increasing educators' knowledge in the professional learning community system.

## Reflective Notes

Which of the policies or infrastructures have you seen implemented in your PLCs?

_____

_____

_____

How have the policies been implemented?

_____

_____

_____

Would you implement the policies differently from your PLCs? Explain

_____

_____

_____

# IDEA FOUR: SYSTEM TRANSFORMATION

An increase in fidelity implementation with evidence-based instruction in the classroom can be addressed by educators utilizing a Professional Learning Community (PLC) approach. The National Research Center on Learning Disabilities (n.d) indicated that fidelity implementation consists of educators conducting evidence-based instruction the way the instruction was intended, as well as educators conducting screening, progress monitoring, and an open decision-making process with consistency.

Also, Laureate Education (2013a) indicated that fidelity implementation includes not only creating a consensus in regards to continuous system improvement process, but also creating a consensus in regards to new systematic change. Harris and Jones (2010) discussed that a PLC consists of educators that share both leadership and a vision. Furthermore, in the same study, Harris and Jones discussed that PLC's educators take on a collective responsibility to not only change, but also improve instruction to increase students' learning performances.

SEDL Advance Research Improving Education (2014a) discussed that a PLC consists of five attributes: supporting and collective leadership, shared creativity, mutual values and visions, supportive environments, and shared individual practice. These attributes are used not only for organizational change, but also to support educators to improve students' learning performance (SEDL Advance Research Improving Education, 2014a). Since fidelity implementation can improve increasing evidence-based instruction to increase students' learning performance and PLCs provide ways for educators to increase students' learning performance, PLCs can continuously support educators with increasing fidelity implementation of evidenced-based instruction.

In PLCs, having a shared vision is an attribute that can assist educators with increasing fidelity implementation of evidenced-based instruction in classrooms. SEDL Advance Research Improving Education (2014) indicated that a shared vision guides the school with not only what is important to the people in the school and what is important to the organization, but also guides the stakeholders with collaborative decision making.

In addition, a PLC's school vision is driven based on the students' learning needs (SEDL Advance Research Improving Education, 2014). In alignment with Laureate Education (2013), SEDL (2014) indicated that a shared vision can assist in identifying the school's population needs, while allowing the educators to build constantly and reflect on practices.

Furthermore, Fullan (2010) discussed that educators of a successful school are always interested in both what intervention is currently working, and in the next effective approach. Therefore, it is important for the leader(s) to ensure that educators are involved in developing a shared vision because the educators can identify the resources needed for continuous improvement for fidelity evidence-based instruction, and address how to use fidelity for evidence-based instruction for constant improvement of students' learning performance. Nevertheless, organizations implementing collaboration, networking and distributed leadership provide means for continuous improvement.

PLC educators can use collaboration, networking, and distributed leadership to sustain continuous improvement of fidelity implementation for evidence-based instruction in regards to increasing students' learning performance. Fullan (2010) discussed that collective capacity building consists of everyone providing different information for a common goal, while everyone takes on the role as co-learners.

Collective capacity supports continuous improvement by ensuring that effective practices are always not only available and accessible, but also ensuring on-going commitment through educators collaborative decision making effort (Fullan, 2010). In other words, everyone in the PLC is continuously committed to being equally responsible and equally accountable for the students' academic success through a continuous collaborative process. Harris and Jones (2010) discussed PLC using networking and collaboration allows for organizational change and improvement.

In addition, Harris and Jones (2010) defined distributed leadership as educators working as equal partners to analyzing a specific topic. In the same 2010 study, Harris and Jones indicated that using a distributed leadership approach provides a way for educators to accomplish continuous improvement. SEDL Advance Research Improving Education (2014) indicated that people in a PLC do not only have expertise in different areas, but also the people in a PLC use their knowledge collectively to determine ways (intervention) to assist students with their learning needs. In order to institute using educators' knowledge to support a common goal, a leader should not only encourage different schools to provide methods for a common goal (within their own schools), but provide a way for each school to collaborate with each other about their methods to support the common goal (i.e., best practice fair). Nevertheless, an organization keeping track of the intended organizational goal is a way for an organization to implement continuous improvement.

Educators assessing the progress of a goal can be a technique to continuously improve fidelity implementation of evidence-based instruction in regards to increasing students' learning performance. Hirsh and Hord (2010) discussed that PLCs can use benchmarks and documentation evidence to determine the goal's level of progress. For this reason, using a rubric as a benchmark tool to determine where the team's level of progress with the implementation of evidenced based fidelity. Furthermore, employing a fidelity checklist to document the level of progress in regards to the implementation with evidence-based fidelity in the classroom. In addition, school teams can apply a rubric and the fidelity checklist during their team meetings to ensure the team is meeting their purpose with fidelity. Therefore, it can be concluded that the rubric and the fidelity checklist can be effective in regards to continuous improvement because it shows the current level of fidelity implementation, and the next step the team needs to take in order to accomplish full fidelity implementation for evidenced-based instruction in the classroom. Besides an organization using measures to assess continuous improvement; there are different ways leaders support an organization can assist with continuous improvement.

There are various ways leaders can support educators in PLCs for continuous improvement of fidelity implementation for evidence-based instruction in regards to increasing students' learning performance. SEDL Advanced Research Improving Education (2014) and Gray, Mitchell, & Tarter, 2014, indicated that a PLC can support on-going organizational change and improvement by implementing effective physical change and people capacity.

Hirsh and Hord (2010) discussed that leaders can provide time for educators to attend professional workshop training and provide time for educators to have follow-up training. Hence, the attaining and the distribution of knowledge is a way for organizations to accomplish continuous improvement (Harris & Jones, 2010).

Therefore, leaders should provide educators with the time to attend fidelity implementation workshops that consist of teams learning about specific and transportable teamwork competencies, (Weaver, Rosen, Salas, Baum, & King, 2010). Hence, teamwork competencies can assist identifying errors in the process of implementing fidelity of evidence-based instruction (due to team members understanding each team members role) for correction purposes (specific teamwork competencies). These teamwork competencies also allow educators the ability to collaborate across and between schools in regards to implementing fidelity of evidence-based instruction for increasing students' learning performance (transportable teamwork competencies).

Leaders should provide coaches or mentors for educators that need the extra support after attending the comprehensive fidelity implementation workshops (Hirsh & Hord, 2010). In addition, leaders should collaborate with team members by instituting professional rules for collaboration. The purpose of these rules is for team members to feel comfortable when expressing themselves at meetings in regards to implementing evidence-based instructional classroom fidelity (Buffum, Mattos & Weber, 2012). Nevertheless, relationships among staff members can affect continuous improvement.

Staff members' relationships in PLCs can be an attributed factor for the continuous improvement of evidence-based fidelity implementation for increasing students' learning performance. Gray et al. (2014) discussed that trust and collective efficacy can affect continuous improvement. The more that staff members trust one another, the higher there is a chance for changes to occur (Gray et al., 2014). Thus, staff would need to trust one another in order for continuous improvement of implementing fidelity for evidenced based classroom instruction.

In addition, the more that teachers believe their colleagues are capable to assist students with positive learning performance results (collective efficacy), the more likely this perception would sustain the efforts to create and retain an effective PLC, and to collectively decide on goals to assist in increasing students' learning performance (Gray et al., 2014). Hence, in order for staff members to continue collective decision making and sustaining effective PLC, it is important for staff members to perceive each other as a valuable resource for information.

PLCs require educators to learn together by collaborating and providing feedback to one another. When educators learn together, they are more likely to base their decision making on facts (Buffum et al., 2012). Therefore, it can be concluded that educator collaboration would assist to build trusting relationships and perceive each other as valuable resources.

Even though this chapter provides ways that PLCs can support fidelity implementation for classroom evidence-based instruction, it is important to remember that the PLC methods would vary for each learning community. The methods in which educators implement methods would also vary, based upon each school's shared vision. Thus, it is suggested that leaders invest in developing positive relationships in order to promote open and honest communication with their PLC educators. This will allow leaders to identify the ways that the leaders can support their PLCs for continuous improvement, while ensuring that the resources would assist with the school's continuous improvement.

### Reflective Notes

How does your PLCs increase fidelity?

_____

_____

_____

Which tool(s) do you find most beneficial for your PLCs to increase fidelity?

_____

_____

_____

How would you use the tools that you find most beneficial, to increase your PLCs fidelity?

_____

_____

_____

# IDEA FIVE: COLLABORATION

## The Importance of Collaboration

Collaboration among educators in a school setting is a key factor that drives effective decision-making. Wilcox and Angelis (2012) indicated that building capacity for a school's decision process includes (a) staff members agreeing to a shared vision, (b) community support, (c) effective programing, (d) administration resource support, and (e) leadership engagement. Therefore, collaboration in a school setting takes on a collective responsibility among teams of educators to increase students' academic skills. Team members share ideas to help guide students towards exhibiting positive social, emotional behaviors. The school's teams consist of school leadership teams, collaborative teacher teams or co-teaching teams, and school intervention teams.

## Role of Collaboration

The problem-solving team's purpose is to collaborate to find scientific evidence-based ideas in order to solve a problem. Buffum et al. (2012) discussed that in order for collaboration to be successful, teams must believe that all children can learn, and believe in the concept of shared responsibility. Shared responsibility occurs when team members believe that everyone is accountable for students' learning outcomes. In order for shared responsibility to be successful, team members must believe in a shared vision, which is that all children can learn.

In addition to shared responsibility and a shared vision, teams that learn together can assist in the decision-making process. Team members, when they are educated about the same concepts, tend to make decisions based on facts. The problem-solving teams are accountable for students' academic and social emotional results, and these teams learn together. Basing decisions on facts and academic and social emotional results are important aspects for decision-making. However, conflict plays a very important role in the problem-solving process.

## Conflict Occurs in all Problem-Solving Decision-Making Processes

Mind Tools (2014) discussed that constructive conflict can be a positive element when teams are coming to an agreement about how to solve a problem. Constructive conflict occurs when teams use others' ideas in order to come to a consensus about constructing an effective solution to a problem. Constructive conflict assists team members in developing close relationships, while promoting effective communication and setting the stage for successfully solving a problem (University of Missouri-St. Louis, 2014). Therefore, teams that use conflict in a constructive way are highly effective in developing a solution in regard to solving problems.

However, team members' personalities play an important role when conflict occurs in regards to teams' solving a problem. Both how team members view conflict and how their views affect the team's performance for solving problems. Huang (2012) discussed that teams with members who possess high learning orientation, or team those who view task conflict as a learning experience, can have a positive effect on the teams' problem-solving performance. During task conflict, team members with elevated learning orientation view other perspectives as a way to increase their knowledge in regard to the teams' targeted performance task.

Cohorts with high learning characteristics are more open to communicating with team members, which can provide the team with more problem-solving options. Therefore, people with learning personalities would be more effective in coming to a consensus with solving a problem because they are capable of collaborating to gain knowledge for effective solutions based on others' viewpoints. However, it is not enough to only have people with learning personalities on a team; creating a professional environment for decision-making can increase problem solving capacity by providing ideas for everyone about effective problem solving methods.

Developing rules for engagement is an important element of effective collaboration, and a team's ability to come to a consensus for solving a problem in a professional manner. Buffum et al. (2012) discussed that it was important to set team norms in order to provide a guideline for how teams should interact with one another.

Professional and positive collaborative guidelines can provide all team members with an opportunity to participate in the conversation, create the atmosphere for all team members to feel comfortable expressing their opinions, and provide the team with an effective schedule. Developing team norms is important for a professional team meeting environment; nevertheless, providing clear roles is equally as important for the organization of team meetings.

The problem-solving team members are assigned to different, clearly-defined roles. Howell et al. (2008) discussed that problem-solving teams should consist of a team leader, a meeting recorder, a timekeeper, a person who manages the data, and a case manager.

## *Problem Solving Team Responsibilities*

| Roles | Responsibilities |
|---|---|
| Team Leader | Providing the professional developments to meet the team's needs, developing team norms, keeping the team focused on the targeted tasks, assigning group responsibilities, and obtaining the group's next step consensus. |
| The Meeting Recorder | Scribing the team's meeting discussions and providing the team meeting with a copy of the team's discussions. |
| Time Keeper | Control the flow of the meeting. |
| Data Manager | Organize the data clearly for team presentation. |
| Case Manager | Should not only be to gather data for progress monitoring purposes, but also interviewing parents and students for data purposes. |

Therefore, the problem-solving team assigning team members' roles would result in a clear and effective organizational environment. However, parents and administrators are important people that should participate in the collaborative efforts for problem-solving.

Howell et al. (2008) discussed that principals and parents are critical to the problem-solving process. A principal's collaborative involvement provides a comprehensive understanding that the RTI's (MTSS) process is pertinent to students' academic and social emotional success. Parents' collaborative involvement can provide the team with different perspectives to address students' learning or behavioral needs. Therefore, it can be concluded that even though principals' and parents' collaboration support the problem-solving process in different ways, the support from both parties provides the team with supplemental ideas to solve the targeted problem.

## Reflective Notes

How does your organization collaborate to solve problems or make decisions?

_____

_____

_____

Which of the concepts in this section align to your PLCs concerning problem solving or decision making?

_____

_____

_____

Which of these concepts can be most beneficial to your organization concerning problem solving or decision making?

_____

_____

_____

# IDEA SIX: ALIGNING SCHOOL TEAMS WITH RTI/MTSS/TIERS

There are a variety of teams in a school setting that are responsible for decision-making in regard to improving students' academic or social-emotional performance. Buffum et al. (2012) discussed that school leadership teams, co-team teaching, and school intervention teams are all used to assist students with learning success in a school. These teams are assigned to a specific tier in order to meet students' learning needs.

### School Leadership Team

A school leadership team is assigned in tier one. The school leadership team decides how to guide the entire school in regard to taking a collective responsibility for student learning. They also decide how to use the school's resources to achieve collective responsibility for student learning.

Collaborative professional development is a way for all educators in the school environment to take on a collective responsibility. One way to provide this is by conducting professional development sessions for each other to learn how to increase students' learning (Waldron & McLeskey, 2010). Collaborative professional development is aligned to tier one because the collaborative professional development would affect all staff members for all students' learning success.

### Collaborative Teacher Team or Co-Teaching Team

A collaborative teacher team or co-teaching team is assigned in tier two. This tier addresses a small group of students with similar learning needs. A collaborative teacher team or co-teaching teams are made up of educators that share the same curriculum and educators that take on collective responsibility approach to implement strategies for a specific group of students that share the same learning needs to be academically and/or social emotionally successful (Friend, Cook, Hurley-Chamberlain & Shamberger, 2010). Co-teaching teams were aligned to tier two because co-teaching teams and the tier two intervention style's purpose is to collaborate on the learning needs of a specific group of students to increase their academic skills.

### School Intervention Team

A school intervention team is assigned in tier three. A school intervention team takes on a collective responsibility approach to focus on an individual student in need of intensive support for academic and/or social emotional success. Therefore, not only do teams share a collective responsibility ethic in order to support students' learning success, but also that different teams are used to make decisions on different levels based on the students' learning needs.

## Reflective Notes

How does your organization assign teams to meet the students' learning needs?

_____

_____

_____

Do you think this is an effective method to address the students' learning needs? Explain.

_____

_____

_____

# IDEA SEVEN: TEAMS AND TIERS: BARRIERS AND ADMINISTRATIVE SOLUTIONS

## Changing School Culture and Barriers

Changing a school's culture can create collaborative barriers. Waldron and Mc Leskey (2010) discussed that barriers can develop when a school's culture changes from using a traditional form of professional development method to a collaborative professional development method. Since collaborative professional development requires more funding and more time, funding scheduling barriers are created that prevent frequent collaborative professional development.

If schools do not possess a collaborative culture, it can cause a barrier for schools to implement collaborative professional developments (due to the staff member not taking ownership in the shared vision). A lack of both active leadership support for collaborative professional developments and administration commitment can cause a capacity building barrier. Thus, staff members with a lack of motivation for collaboration can create barriers in regard to implementing collaborative professional developments in many schools. However, there are varieties of ways to overcome the barriers that prevent collaborative professional developments.

## Plan for Enhancing Collaborative Professional Development

School administrators play an important role in developing a school culture that welcomes collaborative professional development. Waldron and McLeskey (2010) discussed that school administrators' support is an influential factor in creating and sustaining a collaborative culture which in turns sets the stage for collaborative professional development. In addition, a school leader must be knowledgeable about both the meaning of a collaborative culture, and the reason a collaborative culture is important.

Therefore, the level of engagement and the support a school leader provides can determine the level of overall collaboration in a school.

School administrators and/or school leaders can benefit by enhancing professional developments. An active school administrator can provide building school capacity and ensure consistency for collaborative professional development, while developing a collaborative culture. Also, a school administrator can begin by providing the school educators with reasons why collaborative professional developments are beneficial and how it would assist the educators in helping the students. In addition, a school administrator can develop a school leadership team to address creating collaborative professional developments. Moreover, a school administrator who supports distributed leadership can provide teachers with ownership in implementing collaborative professional developments, and with support in changing from traditional professional developments to collaborative professional developments.

Likewise, a school administrator on a school leadership team can provide support to the team in regard to staying on topic to ensure clear decisions about professional development activities. They can create a schedule that provides time for more collaborative professional developments and the needed funding for collaborative professional developments. Besides, a school leader can set a professional tone for staff members collaborating on developing professional norms for collaboration. Conjointly, a school leader and the school leadership team can decide on user-friendly and effective forms to use for collaborative efforts. Furthermore, a school leader should provide professional development for the school leadership team, in order for the school leadership team to be able to make knowledgeable school decisions. Lastly, a school leader can provide the school leadership team with time to collaborate.

* See what a school administrator does by looking at the chart below. *

| School Administrator (team) | School Administrator (solo) |
|---|---|
| Support team with staying on topic | Provide building school capacity |
| Ensure clear decisions about professional development activities | Ensure consistency for collaborative professional development |
| Create schedules | Develop a collaborative culture |
| Decide on user-friendly forms, professional development opportunities, and length of time | Provide reasons why collaborative professional developments are useful and important |
| Sets professional tone with team members | Provide ownership and support to teachers |

## Co-Teaching Team Barriers

Co-teaching teams have a variety of collaborative barriers. Pugach and Winn (2011) discussed that barriers to collaboration may be caused by administrators not supporting co-teacher teams and educators not volunteering for a co-teaching team assignment.

Administrators that do not provide support for co-teaching teams can result in these teams not collaborating enough, due to a lack of time. Additionally, it can result in a deficit of knowledge for the special education teacher, which would not allow the two teachers to collaborate as effectively. Finally, if this co-teaching assignment is forced on one or both partners, a lack of ownership and commitment to collective responsibility for student learning needs can occur.

Even though there are a multitude of barriers that can prevent the success of co-teaching in schools, there are also strategies that can be implemented to address these collaborative barriers.

## Plan for Enhancing Co-Teaching Teams.

Administrators supporting co-teacher teams can help to overcome barriers. Pugach and Winn (2011) indicated that support from school leaders can provide guidance for co-teaching teams, and can assist the educators in providing high-quality support for the students. Thus, administrators carefully selecting teachers based on compatibility, content knowledge, and teaching methodologies can not only create a successful co-teaching team, but also reduce co-teaching stress.

- Teachers with compatible personalities who are involuntarily assigned to the co-teaching team would most likely develop a trusting and respectful connection for effective collaboration.

- Providing targeted professional development for special education teachers and general education teachers would support them in regard to the same content knowledge, and create an equal instructional environment.
- Administrators that schedule planning time for co-teaching educators to collaborate can result in educators determining equal classroom teaching opportunities and allow for co-teaching educators to attend meetings that apply to their co-teaching assignments.

In addition to administrators supporting co-teachers through compatibility selection, it is also important for administrators to support co-teachers through providing different team collaborative structures.

There are a variety of ways to create meetings for co-teacher teams to collaborate."Buffum et al. (2012) discussed multiple ways for co-teachers to collaborate.

- The grade level meetings, which address educators who teach at the same grade level.
- The subject/course specific teams meetings, which address educators who teach the same course/subject.
- The vertical collaborative teams meetings, which address educators that are responsible for learning outcomes that develop within a set amount of years. For example: Fourth grade math team discusses standards and objectives with a fifth grade math team.
- The interdisciplinary collaborative teams meetings, which consist of teachers who teach the same students, but different subjects.

Therefore, by providing tier two teaching teams with the tools necessary for collaboration, it would allow educators to determine ways to assist students with increasing their learning needs. However, for students who are not responding to the tier two agreed interventions, educators would need to collaborate based on the individual student's learning needs.

## Collaborative Barriers for a School Intervention Team

Tier three addresses the students with the most severe academic and/or social emotional needs. Sulkowski, Wingfield, Jones, and Coulter (2011) indicated that the lack of collaboration among team members and outside professionals can cause a lack of information about individual students. In the same 2011 study, Sulkowski et al. mention that the process for obtaining information from team members and outside professionals can be cumbersome. Having an unorganized process in regard to collecting information can cause a barrier for addressing students' educational or social emotional needs:

- The process of parents signing consent forms in order for a student's information to be shared among outside professionals and school intervention team members can slow the information process and take a long time to obtain.
- The process of outside professionals receiving the consent forms and sending the needed information to the team can slow down the information process and take a long time to obtain. The process of identifying and updating expired records can also slow down the information process.
- The process of filing the shared records can be tedious. Members of the school's intervention team, the outside professionals, and/or the parents not

attending the meetings could interfere with sharing information about the student's learning needs.

The process of obtaining and taking care of records can cause barriers in the collaborative process if they are not performed in a timely and efficient manner. However, in order to provide individual students with effective interventions; the process of obtaining information and keeping the information current must be done smoothly and efficiently.

## *Plan for Enhancing Collaboration in a School Intervention Team*

A tier three school intervention team can overcome the slow process of collecting information. Sulkowski et al. (2011) indicated that pinpointing one person to monitor collecting information would support the information process by hiring an individualized education plan (IEP) coordinator. That person would be responsible for:

- Identifying expired consent forms
- Sending out consent forms to outside professionals and parents
- Keeping track of unreturned consent forms.
- Contacting outside professionals and/or parents for reminders about returning consent forms
- Reminding the school intervention team, the parents and the outside professionals about scheduled meetings.
- Assisting with storing students' information in a central file for easy access.

## Reflective Notes

Does your organization have collaborative team barriers?

_____

_____

_____

What type of collaborative team barriers, if any, does your organization face?

_____

_____

_____

How does your organization solve collaborative team barriers?

_____

_____

_____

Why do you think the collaborative team barriers exist (if any) in your organization?

_____

_____

_____

How would you solve the collaborative team barrier(s) in your organization?

_____

_____

_____

# IDEA EIGHT: DISCUSSING FIDELITY IMPLEMENTATION

### The Importance of Discussing Implementing With Fidelity in PLC

The focus of this literature review is to demonstrate ways to increase students' learning performance through implementing with fidelity in regards to evidence-based classroom instruction. Traditionally, implementing with fidelity has been defined as the degree of adherence to an instructional plan (Cook & Smith, 2012; Harn, Parisi & Stoolmiller, 2013; Kutash, Cross, Madias, Duchnowski, 2012 & Green, 2012).

Currently, the definition of implementation with fidelity has been extended to treatment exposure, treatment quality or competence, program differentiation, participant exposure, and participant responsiveness (Cook & Smith, 2012; Harn, Parisi & Stoolmiller, 2013; Kutash et al., 2012). For this reason, this section will provide research literature that supports implementing with fidelity for increasing evidence-based instruction.

### Theories and Fidelity

Implementing a program with fidelity is the central component of sustainability. Fidelity implementation is affected by regeneration (Mcintosh, MacKay, Hume, Doolittle, Vincent, Horner, & Ervin, 2011). Herlo (2010) discussed that transformative learning occurs when educators collaborate and use the perspectives from one another to develop a new point of reference. Mason (2009) discussed that complexity theory consists of constitutions interacting with one another and, as a result, an unexpected behavior emerges. However, that unexpected behavior's power behind its momentum affects other elements in its path (Mason, 2009).

If the unexpected behavior receives positive feedback, it can result in the unexpected behavior being sustained (Mason, 2009). Thus, educators' collaborative efforts can sustain implementation with fidelity for evidence-based instruction in the classroom by providing evidence-based intervention instruction based on the students' learning performance needs.

However, if the students' present level of performance changes, then the educators would need to collaborate again in order to find another evidence-based instruction method to support the students' new learning needs. This is similar to how unexpected behavior can change paths if interacting with another continuant.

### *Measurements to Determine the Degree of Implementing with Fidelity*

Mcintosh's et al. (2011) research study's purpose was to measure the validity and the reliability of School-Wide Universal Behavior Sustainability Index-School Teams (SUBSIST). The SUBSIST determines the elements that improved or prevented the sustainability for School-Wide Positive Behavior Support intervention. The elements were (a) priority, (b) effectiveness (c) efficiency, (d) and continuous regeneration. Continuous regeneration divided into the use of data and building capacity. Administrative leadership was divided into building and external leadership subscales.

The SUBSIST measure was associated with the school's fidelity implementation for the current school year. Content validity was used to obtain information from an expert panel in regards to each element on the SUBSIST and the SUBSIST as a whole. The Content Validity Index (CVI) was used to quantify the results in regards to the degree that each item and the entire measurement were characterized in the construct of sustainability. The School-Wide Evaluation Tool (SETS) was used as an outside measurement tool to examine the school's universal School Wide Positive Behavior Intervention and Support (SWPBIS) system.

The Cronbach's alpha coefficient was used to test various forms of internal consistency. The results of Cronbach's alpha coefficient indicated that .95 reliability in regards to the coaches' and team leaders' interrater reliability. This indicated a moderate relation with fidelity implementation for the assessed school year.

Also, the results indicated that the SUBSIST was a reliable and valid measurement tool for evaluating factors for sustainability. Therefore, it is not only important to measure the implementation with fidelity, but also it is important to ensure that the statistical measures used are valid and reliable.

Just like Mcintosh's et al. (2011) research study, Debnam's, Pas' and Bradshaw's (2012) research study discussed SWPBIS. However, Debnam's et al. (2012) research study purpose was to provide a comprehensive understanding of the types and features of supports that are commonly utilized by educational institutions effectively implementing SWPBIS.

Debman et al. (2012) examined the types and features of supports that are commonly utilized by schools effectively implementing SWPBIS by (a) identifying schools that were implementing the universal support tier, but had educators that were not trained in tiers 2 and 3, (b) examining the levels of support needed for tiers 2 and 3 in relation to implementation of fidelity for SWPBIS model and to a set of school demographic characteristics, and (c) describing the three most commonly used intervention attributes for tier two programs. The researchers obtained the school's demographics from the Maryland State Department of Education (Debnam et al., 2012).

School-Wide Evaluation Tool (SET) was used to test the degree to which the school implemented the important features of SWPBIS (Debnam et al., 2012). The researchers used the Individual Student System Evaluation Tool (I-SSET) to document the characteristics of tiers 2 and 3 support services utilized in the educational facility for the implementation of SWPBIS (Debnam et al., 2012). The training of the assessor consisted of (a) reviewing the training manual, (b) attended a half day SET/I-SSET training sessions taught by a lead SET/I-SSET training staff, and (c) shadowed the lead SET/I-SSET trainer in a full assessment of a non-project SWPBIS elementary school (Debnam et al., 2012).

After training the assessors, they assessed using the SET/I-SSET in a project SWPBIS elementary school (Debnam et al., 2012). The research study resulted showed that there was an increase in the degree of implementation for the SWPBIS features, the percentage of schools scored a two for full implementation of SWPBIS supports, and the most commonly used characteristics used in the tier 2 intervention were the interventions was directly linked to school-wide interventions and students' obtaining positive feedback from staff (Debnam et al., 2012). Even though both Debnam's et al. (2012) research study and Mcintosh's et al. (2011) research study utilized statistical measures to demonstrate the degree for the implementation with fidelity, there are other ways to measure the degree for the implementation with fidelity.

In contrast to Mcintosh's et al. (2011) research study and Debnam's et al. (2012) research study, Century, Rudnick and Freeman's (2010) research study utilized a different method for measuring the degree to which fidelity was implemented. Century's et al. (2010) research study discussed not only developing a framework for measuring the implementation with fidelity, but also how the framework can be used to support the measurement for implementation with fidelity in regards to evidence-based intervention across various programs. This research study provided a definition for fidelity with implementation, structural critical component, instructional critical components, aligned the framework with previous works, and ways that the framework can be used.

Mcintosh et al. (2011), Debnam et al. (2012) and Century et al. (2010) explored measuring the implementation with fidelity. Mcintosh et al. (2011) and Debnam et al. (2012) used SETS to measure the degree to which the components of the SWPBIS were implemented with fidelity. Also, Debnam et al. (2011) and Mcintosh et al. (2011) used additional different measurements to assist with measuring the implementation with fidelity. Debnam et al. (2011) additional measurement was Individual Student System Evaluation Tool (I-SSET) and Mcintosh et al. (2012) additional measurements were Content Validity Index (CVI) and Cronbach's alpha coefficients. Century's et al. (2010) research study was different from Debnam's et al (2011) research study and Mcintosh's et al. (2012) research study because Century et al. (2010) developed a framework in order to measure the implementation with fidelity.

Debnam's et al. (2011) and Mcintosh's et al. (2012) research study yielded similar results because the two research studies focused on SWPBIS. Even though each of the research study's purposes was different, all of the research studies provided measurements not only of the degree for the implementation with fidelity, but also identified critical components (features) that were necessary for effective degree of implementation.

In addition, by Mcintosh et al. (2011), Debnam et al (2012), and Century et al. (2010) measuring the degree of the implementation with fidelity would assist in determining that the program used to increase students' learning performance can be a product of a flawed program and not the students' learning ability (National Center for Learning Disabilities, n.d).

### Conceptual Frameworks and Implementation with Fidelity

Professional learning communities, response to intervention, and positive behavioral intervention and support have a system that requires educators to implement fidelity in order to sustain continuous improvement for students' learning performance.

Professional learning communities are required to use collaboration to determine the students' present level of performance, and to determine the intervention necessary to improve the students' learning performance (Harris & Jones, 2010; SEDL Advance Research Improving Education, 2014).

In addition, if the intervention that was recommended by educators is not meeting the students' needs, the educators must collaborate again to adjust the intervention or find a different intervention (Hirsh & Hord, 2010). Just like professional learning communities, response to intervention requires educators to collaborate in order to make a decision based on the intervention that would support the students' academic needs (Buffum, Mattos & Weber, 2012; RTI Action Network, 2015; The University of the State of New York & The State Education Department, 2010).

Similar to professional learning communities, response to intervention requires the educators to reconvene if the intervention proposed is not meeting the students' learning needs and to change the intervention is necessary (Buffum, Mattos and Weber, 2012; RTI Action Network, 2015; The University of the State of New York & The State Education Department, 2010). Positive behavioral interventions and support systems require educators to collaborate in order to determine interventions to support the improvement of students' social-emotional needs (Positive Behavioral Interventions and Supports, 2015). Just like professional learning communities and response to intervention, positive behavioral interventions and support systems require educators to meet if the decided intervention is not helping the student improve their social-emotional needs (Positive Behavioral Interventions and Supports, 2015).

Response to intervention and positive behavioral interventions support systems are similar due to the fact that degree of level of intervention support is based on the tier (Deshler & Cornett, 2012; Positive Behavioral Interventions and Supports, 2015; RTI Action Network, 2015). Even though each program has different intervention purposes, it is important for the implementation with fidelity to be incorporated in the system's process in determining the appropriate intervention to sustain and support continuous learning.

### Teacher Efficiency, Implementation with Fidelity, and Students' Achievement

Research studies have indicated that not only does teacher efficiency affect fidelity implication, and students' achievement. Teacher efficiency can be defined as an educators' belief about their ability to impact students' learning (Cantrell, Almasi, Carter & Rintamaa, 2013). Implementation with fidelity can be defined as the degree to which educators implement evidence-based instruction as intended (Bumen, Cakar & Yildiz, 2014). Cantrell's et al.

(2013) research study addressed the degree to which teachers' efficiency and implementation with fidelity affected students' achievement. The research studies participants were sixth-grade students and ninth-grade students struggling readers. The results indicated that the students who achieved the highest reading scores were the students with teachers who used a high degree of implementation with fidelity and teacher efficiency (Cantrell et al., 2013).

Azano, Missett, Callahan, Oh, Brunner, Foster, and Moon (2011) investigated the relationship between the implementation with fidelity and students' achievement in relation to a third-grade curriculum. The results of this research study indicated that the teachers' beliefs and experiences affected the implementation with fidelity (Azano et al., 2013). In addition, the results of this research study indicated that students who were taught by teachers that implemented the third-grade curriculum with high fidelity impacted students' achievement scores in a positive way (Azano et al. 2013).

Bumen et al. (2014) discussed factors that affect curriculum in the Turkish cultural context through a literature review. This research's results indicated that teachers' characteristics related to not only teacher efficiency, but also the implementation with fidelity affects curriculum fidelity in a Turkish cultural context. Hence, high teacher efficiency and high implementation with fidelity most likely produce high student achievement, and low teacher efficiency and low implementation with fidelity would most likely produce low student achievement.

Thus, administrators providing professional developments to increase educators' knowledge about the implementation with fidelity for evidence-based instruction, will not only increase teacher's efficiency, but also positively affect a students' learning performance.

## Dose, Quality, Adaptation, Participants' Responsiveness and Implementation with Fidelity

Kutash's et al. (2012) research study discussed features of the implementation with fidelity that are also discussed in Mainieri and Anderson's (2015) research study to support increasing evidence-based instruction. Kutash et al. (2012) discussed that dose (frequency), quality of delivery, participants' responsiveness and adaptation can be factors to address in regards to the implementation with fidelity not only improving the Teens Leading and Connecting Program (TLC), but also to identify the mechanisms and features that affect implementation.

Mainieri 's and Anderson's (2015) research study, discussed using dose, quality of delivery and participants' responsiveness as implementation with fidelity features to support improving evidence-based practices for a children's mental health program. In Kutash's et al. (2012) research study, dose was referred to as the amount of time the participants met with the parent coordinator. In Mainieri's and Anderson's (2015) research study, dose was referred to the length of time in between the adaptation feature and the duration of the research study.

| Kutash's et al. (2012) Study | Mainier's and Anderson's (2015) Study |
|---|---|
| Quality of delivery was referred to as continuous supervision and support provided by the parent connectors. | Quality of delivery was mentioned as the degree to which the TLC program was intended to be implemented. |

| | |
|---|---|
| *Participants' responsiveness was referred to as the number of contacts between the parents and the parent coordinator, the participants' rating of helpfulness in regards to the parent connectors' intervention, and rating the participants' satisfactory response with the program.* | *Participants' responsiveness was referred to as the engagement level of the participants in the TLC program.* |
| *Adaptation was referred to as changing a feature to enhance the program.* | |

Kutash's et al. (2012) and Mainieri and Anderson (2015) used dose, quality of delivery and participants' responsiveness as implementation of fidelity features to increase participants' knowledge of the targeted program. However, Mainieri's and Anderson's (2015) and Kutash's et al. (2012) research studies are different because Marinier and Anderson (2015) added an adaptation implementation with fidelity feature to their research study in order for the intervention to fit the TLC program.

### Adherence, Dose, Quality of Delivery and Participants' Responsiveness.

Coaches and educators provided collective feedback with one another to improve fidelity application for evidence-based instruction (Deshler & Cornett, 2012). Coaching can be described as a way to provide personalized instructional information to educators, and for specific classroom conditions (Powell & Diamond, 2013).

Powell's and Diamond's (2013) research study examined the implementation with fidelity of an early literacy and language professional development (PD) program for Head Start educators provided by onsite coach visits to classrooms, coaches feedback on teacher-submitted videotapes of specified instructional practices (remote) and access to hypermedia resources (video library). This research study was based on three features of the conceptual coaching framework: structural domain, process domain, and content domain (Powell & Diamond, 2013). Kutash's et al. (2012) research study's purpose was to decrease the implementation gap in children's mental health services through the implementation with fidelity to increase evidence-based practices. Kutash et al. (2012) discussed that adherence, quality of delivery and participants' responsiveness can be utilized as a feedback feature for researchers to comprehend efficiency, and as monitoring features to provide feedback to implementers.

| Powell's and Diamond's (2013) Research Study | In Kutash's et al. (2012) Research Study |
|---|---|
| The structural domain was referred to as the length of coaching and the amount of coaching (dose). | The dose was referred to as the length of time the participants spoke with the parent connector. |
| The process domain was referred to as the performance feedback about the teacher's practices and the coaches' recommendation feedback, and as the degree of educators' involvement in coaching sessions and the educators' perception in regards to the coaches' helpful | The quality of delivery was referred to as the continuous support and supervision that was given to the Parent Connector by the Parent Connector coach. |

| | |
|---|---|
| *characteristics (quality of delivery).* | |
| *Content domain was described as the evidence-based practice used to increase students' learning performance.* | *The evidence-based program that was used to support families was the Family Connector Program.* |
| *The adherence of the coaching protocol can be described as observing the educators' instructional practices based on the coaching schedule, using the fidelity checklist to evaluate the educators' practices, and providing the educators with feedback based on their implementation of practices.* | *Adherence was referred to as the degree to which the Parent Connector's intervention was delivered.* |

Even though the research studies used the same features for the implementation with fidelity and used coaches as a way to provide the implementation with fidelity features, the research studies applied these features based on not only the interventions' purpose, but also based on the research study's intended outcome results.

### *Tracking Forms, Videos, Coaching, Data Driven Instruction and Implementing with Fidelity*

Bianco's (2010) research study examined utilizing coaching, video clips and intervention tracking forms to enhance fidelity for data driven instruction. Just like Powell's and Diamond's (2013) research study, Bianco (2010) utilized a coach to support teachers who were having difficulty with implementing fidelity in alignment to intervention adherence. However, in Bianco's (2010) research study, the coach was used to support the teachers who did not record the intervention video and had difficulty with a students' lack of progress.

Kretlow, Cookes and Wood's (2012) research study discussed providing professional developments to support educators with fidelity for evidence-based classroom instruction, and using coaches for educators that needed additional support with implementing fidelity for evidence-based classroom instruction. Kretlow's et al. (2012) research study was different from Bianco's (2010) research study because Kretlow's et al (2012) research study used coaching as a supplemental support for educators that went to a professional development.

Powell's and Diamond's (2013) research study and Bianco's (2010) research study both used technology as a tool to assist teachers' in regards to applying fidelity. However, in Bianco's (2010) research study, a video was used to instruct teachers on learning how to implement specific elements in regards to data-driven research-based instruction. In Powell's and Diamond's (2013) research study, a video was used to provide teachers with feedback based on the teachers' using fidelity in their delivery of instruction.

Swain's, Finney's, and Gerstner's (2013) and Bianco's (2010) research study discussed using a fidelity checklist to ensure that fidelity was implemented for evidence-based instruction (intervention). For this reason, fidelity checklists, videos, and coaches can be used to support educators with fidelity implementation not only to increase students' learning performances, but also to support educators' knowledge of instructional adherence.

This literature review aligned evidence-based research studies concerning fidelity implementation features to demonstrate how the fidelity's implementation features can be used to support increasing evidence-based instruction. Many of the evidence-based research studies used fidelity implemented features together. In addition, statistical measurements have been identified as to whether it can be either the same or different in order to measure the degree of fidelity application in regards to evidence-based practices.

Also, implementing fidelity can be used across different programs to increase students' learning performance. Since the features for implementing with fidelity can be used in a variety of ways based on the intervention, I would suggest that an administrators and staff members should take into account the implemented fidelity features that would support increasing evidence-based classroom instruction and the measurement tools used to identify the degree to which the fidelity was implemented.

## Reflective Notes

Which research study do you feel would be most effective to assist with improving your organization's PLCs implementation with fidelity for student improvement? Explain.

_____

_____

_____

Which research study is in alignment with your organization's PLCs fidelity methods for student improvement? Explain.

_____

_____

_____

# IDEA NINE: PROGRAM ASSESSMENT

The implementation of different evaluation methods ensure that the PLC is continuously using the professional infrastructures to not only sustain educators' learning process, but also that the educator's knowledge evolves to support students' learning needs. Some evaluation methods are (Mertens & Wilsons, 2012):

| |
|---|
| *Building Capacity Evaluation* – Support planning for the program |
| *Needs Assessment Evaluation* – provide the resources that the PLC program needs, and that the PLC has to support the existing program |
| *Replication/Transportability/Exportability* Evaluation – assist with indicating if effective elements from another program can be used in this PLC program |
| *Monitoring Evaluation* – ensure that the PLC program is being conducted with adherence for effective outcomes |
| *Developmental Evaluation* – assist the PLC with indicating if any adjustments are needed due to environmental changes or program subtleties |
| *Implementation Evaluation* – support if the aims of the PLC program have been attained |
| *Sustainability Evaluation* – conducted every two years to ensure that PLC has maintained a continuous systematic method after the funds have depleted |

Therefore, implementing evaluations will assist with ensuring that the PLC is continuously keeping abreast with the new educational practices.

The implementation with fidelity for increasing evidence-based classroom instruction can be described as providing evidence-based instruction as the way it was intended to be implemented (The National Research Center on Learning Disabilities, n.d). Evidence-based instruction can be described as the degree of rigor used to prove that the intervention (educational practice) was effective (U.S. Department of Education, 2003). However, it is important to employ fidelity for increasing evidence-based classroom instruction, and to ensure that the fidelity for increasing evidence-based classroom instruction is continuously sustained.

Walden University (2013) indicated that continuous improvement occurs when a person provides a system for continuous improvement. Thus, implementing fidelity for increasing evidence-based instruction, a system would need to be designed to continuously support employing fidelity for increasing evidence-based classroom instruction. Even though a system has been put in place for continuous improvement for applying fidelity for increasing evidence-based classroom instruction, it is necessary to sustain the system for fidelity implementation for increasing evidence-based classroom instruction.

Coffey and Horner (2012) discussed that the features to sustain continuous improvement for fidelity practices are (a) contextual appropriate innovation, (b) a shared vision, (c) administrative supports, (c) leadership at various levels, (d) on-going technical assistance, (e) data-driven instructional decision making, and (f) continuous regeneration. Evaluations are used for identifying the needs of a program, evaluating the context of a program, building a program capacity, evaluating and monitoring the program's process and sustainability. Putting an evaluation system in place, with fidelity, would support continuous improvement for increasing evidence-based classroom instruction.

The focus of this section is to identify effective evaluation strategies that would support the implementation with fidelity for increasing evidence-based classroom instruction. The following effective evaluation strategies were (a) implementation evaluation, (b) responsive evaluation, (c) evaluation monitoring, (d) developmental evaluation (e) capacity building evaluation, (f) sustainability evaluation, and (g) replication / exportability / transferability evaluation.

To determine effective evaluation strategies regarding implementing with fidelity for increasing evidence-based classroom instruction, the features for effective implementation with fidelity were aligned with the appropriate, effective evaluation strategy. To support that the increase of evidence-based classroom instruction was the result of the rigorous implementation with fidelity, elements that determine the rigor for the implementation of educational practices to effective evaluation strategies were aligned.

## *Capacity Building Evaluation*

A capacity building evaluation can support the implementation of fidelity for increasing evidence-based classroom instruction. Mertens and Wilson (2012) discussed that a capacity building evaluation can assist with planning in regards to implementing an intervention. A capacity building evaluation can indicate the stakeholders that would be involved in implementing an intervention, and can identify the degree of knowledge the stakeholders have or need in order to implement the intervention (Mertens & Wilson, 2012).

Fullan (2007) discussed that a successful building capacity plan must be purposeful, comprehensible, and organized.

Cook and Smith (2012) discussed that program differentiation and program competence as features of the implementation of fidelity.

Program differentiation is described as only using planned elements of a specific intervention (Cook & Smith, 2012). Program competence is described as the degree of knowledge a stakeholder has in regards to the intervention (Cook & Smith, 2012). Thus, these features can assist the evaluator with not only identifying the specific elements needed for the implementation of fidelity, but also determining what the stakeholders need to learn or already know in order to implement with fidelity.

In addition, the U.S Department of Education (2003) discussed that for the selected intervention to be effective, stakeholders should plan to ensure the participants' characteristics (in the selected research study) and the setting in which the intervention took place (in the selected research study) is similar to the school using the preferred intervention.

Therefore, a building capacity evaluation would support an evaluator's plan for the implementation of fidelity for increasing evidence-based instruction in the following ways:

- An evaluator can determine if the stakeholders have knowledge about the implementation of fidelity for increasing evidence-based instruction.
- An evaluator can determine if the stakeholders have knowledge in regards to identifying evidence-based interventions.
- An evaluator can determine if the stakeholders have the knowledge to align the intervention to the school's characteristics for effective intervention outcomes.
- An evaluator can determine the stakeholders that would be involved in implementing with fidelity for increasing evidence-based classroom instruction.

- An evaluator can determine the resources needed to build the organization capacity for fidelity implementation for increasing evidence-based classroom instruction.

## Implementation Evaluation and Employing Fidelity

The implementation evaluation can be used as an evaluation method for increasing the implementation of evidence-based classroom instruction. The implementation evaluation is used when an existing program or a new program is identified, through data, as having difficulty achieving its goal (Mertens & Wilson, 2012). The implementation evaluation can assist a new or existing program through the following ways (Mertens & Wilson, 2012):

- Determining the program's strengths and weaknesses in regards to the implementation of the targeted program.
- Re-evaluating the appropriateness of the program under different conditions.
- Examining the extent to which the applicable resources were accessible.
- Measuring how the stakeholders perceived the program.
- Determining the service quality of the program.
- Monitoring the stakeholders' experiences with the program.

Validity and reliable outcomes measures are a result of providing not only accurate, but also true outcomes in regards to the effect of the intervention (U.S Department of Education, 2003). Thus, the implementation evaluation measures the degree of effectiveness of an implemented program and the outcome of a program is aligned to how effective fidelity was applied to supported increasing evidence-based classroom instruction (Century, Rudnick & and Freeman, 2010). Therefore, the data from the implementation evaluation would support determining the fidelity application degree of effectiveness for increasing evidence-based classroom instruction.

## Responsive Evaluation and Implementing with Fidelity

A responsive evaluation, when implemented with fidelity, can support increasing evidence-based instruction. A responsive evaluation consists of the on-going feedback to stakeholders (Martens & Wilson, 2012).

Cook and Smith (2012) discussed that an effective feature, when implemented with fidelity, is participants' responsiveness. Kustash, Cross, Madis, Duchnowski, and Green (2012) discussed that participants' responsiveness can determine the degree to which the participants felt that the intervention met their needs and the degree of the participants' engagement. In addition, the U.S Department of Education (2003) suggested that to ensure the self-reporting results from the participants' are valid, a researcher should find an additional way to support the accuracy of the participants' self-reporting results.

Therefore, a responsive evaluation, that is implemented with fidelity can support increasing evidence-based classroom instruction in the following ways:

- The evaluator and the participants can continuously collaborate (with fidelity) the evaluation's outcomes that supports the organizational needs concerning increasing evidence-based classroom instruction (Mainiteri & Anderson, 2015).
- The evaluator can measure the participants' degree of engagement (using the Youth Program Quality

Assessment (YPQA)) in regards to applying fidelity for increasing evidence-based classroom instruction (Mainiteri & Anderson, 2015).

## Monitoring, Adherence, and Implementing with Fidelity

Monitoring can be an effective evaluation strategy with fidelity for increasing evidence-based classroom instruction. Mertens and Wilson (2012) discussed monitoring as continuous assessment of a program's progress through the implementation of the program. Kustash et al. (2012) described adherence as implementing the intervention to the degree in which the intervention was designed. Bumen, Cakar, and Yildiz (2014) described the fidelity implementation as the way to determine how well an intervention was implemented as compared to its initial program's plan. Cook and Smith (2012) identified adherences as an effective feature when fidelity is implemented. U.S Department of Education (2003) discussed that when an evidence-based intervention is conducted with adherence, the evidence-based intervention would have a positive effect on classroom instruction. For this reason, a monitoring strategy would support the implementation of fidelity for increasing evidence-based classroom instruction in the following ways:

- The evaluator can assess the degree of adherence in regards to fidelity implementation for increasing evidence-based classroom instruction.
- The evaluator can determine that the positive effect of fidelity implementation for increasing evidence-based classroom instruction was due to the adherence.

## Developmental Evaluation and Implementing with Fidelity

A developmental evaluation that applies fidelity implementation could be used for increasing evidence-based classroom instruction. Mertens and Wilson (2012) discussed that a developmental evaluation occurs when an evaluator continuously assesses a program for the purpose of adapting elements within the program to enhance the program's outcomes. Skaiski and Romero (2011) discussed that evaluators use formative evaluations (throughout a program) to adjust instruction and interventions.

Cook and Smith (2012) discussed that program differentiation is a feature, when applied with fidelity, can be described as using elements from an evidence-based intervention (depending on the conditions) to enhance the outcome of a targeted program. Hence, only elements from fidelity implemented interventions that can increase evidence-based classroom instruction would be the preferred components.

The U.S Department of Education (2003) discussed that the educators should track data over time to ensure that the preferred choice of evidence-based intervention is providing the same results for the students' in the school (using the preferred choice evidence-based intervention) as the participants in the evidence-based research study. For this reason, a developmental evaluation, that employs fidelity, can be used to support increasing evidence-based classroom instruction in the following manner:

- The evaluator can track, with fidelity, the program's performance data over time to ensure that intervention adjustments are made to support increasing evidence-based classroom instruction.

## Sustainability Evaluation

Sustainability evaluations, that are implemented with fidelity, can be used for increasing evidence-based classroom instruction. Mertens and Wilson (2012) discussed that a sustainability evaluation determines if an organization has a continuous institutionalized, systematic process that supports a program after the external supports (donor supports) are no longer available.

Also, sustainability evaluations usually take place approximately two years after the implementation of the program (Mertens & Wilson, 2012). Treatment exposure and participants' exposure are features implemented with fidelity that can be aligned to sustainability evaluations (Smith & Cook, 2012). Treatment exposure is a feature implemented with fidelity defined as the length of intervention sessions (Smith & Cook, 2012). Hence, treatment exposure and the intervention time length should be aligned.

Participants' exposure is the amount of intervention that a participant received (Smith & Cook, 2012). Hence, participants' exposure should occur when the organization is providing knowledge regeneration to staff members for sustainability purposes (Coffey & Horner, 2012).

Also, the U.S Department of Education (2003) discussed that long-term outcome measures are important because it would determine if the effects of the intervention were sustained. Therefore, sustainability evaluations, when implemented with fidelity, can support increasing evidence-based instruction in the following manner:

- Since fidelity implementation features are associated with the amount of time and the length of exposure, an evaluator can align these features to demonstrate the program's strength in regards to continuous improvement of staff members' knowledge concerning implementing with fidelity for increasing evidence-based classroom instruction.

- The evaluator can also align the programs' strength in regards to maintaining the implementation with fidelity for increasing evidence-based classroom instruction.
- The evaluator can determine if the organization has put into place a systematic fidelity implemented process for sustaining increasing evidence-based classroom instruction.
- The evaluator can determine if the implemented fidelity intervention has a permanent effect on educators increasingly implementing evidence-based classroom instruction.

## Replication / Exportability / Transferability and Implementation With Fidelity

Replication / exportability / transferability evaluations can support the implementation with fidelity for increasing evidence-based classroom instruction. Mertens and Wilson (2012) discussed that a replication / exportability / transferability evaluation's purpose is to determine if a particular program can be transferred to another setting.

In order for a particular program to be deemed as transferable, an evaluator would need to take into consideration not only critical contextual factors that may enhance or not strengthen the replication of the program, but also the chosen communities contextual conditions (Mertens & Wilson, 2012). Program differentiation is a feature (when implemented with fidelity) that can be aligned to a replication/exportability/transferability evaluation. Smith and Cook (2012) discussed that program differentiation consists of using only evidence-based intervention elements that support the chosen setting conditions for the particular program.

The U.S Department of Education (2003) discussed that intervention outcomes for one site are related to the factors of that particular site. Also, it is possible that if the interventions were used on another site, the interventions' outcomes would be different due to the site's factors not being the same (U.S Department of Education, 2003). Therefore, replication / exportability / transferability evaluations can support employing fidelity for increasing evidence-based classroom instruction in the following way:

- The evaluator can investigate if the intended evidence-based program shares not only the same critical contextual factors, but also the same community's contextual conditions in order for effective transferability when it is implemented with fidelity for increasing evidence-based instruction.

## Reflective Notes

Does your organization implement a program assessment?

_____

_____

_____

Which program assessment component(s) do they use?

_____

_____

_____

How does your organization implement the program assessment components?

_____

_____

_____

Which program assessment components do you think would most benefit your organization? Explain.

_____

_____

_____

# IDEA TEN: BEING CULTURALLY DIVERSE

## *Culturally-Diverse Backgrounds Communication Barriers*

In order to support the learning needs of diverse students, it is important for educators to understand the students' culture. Jong (2011) discussed that collaborative barriers have been created in regard to communicating about students' learning needs from culturally-diverse and linguistically-diverse backgrounds. A communication barrier that has been constructed is that parents from culturally-diverse backgrounds rarely exercise their rights to provide their opinion about their child's learning needs (Jong, 2011). Hence, the lack of parents from culturally-diverse backgrounds participation can be due to the parents' culture of trusting the educators with their children's educational needs.

Some parents from culturally-diverse backgrounds feel that educators have a negative attitude towards them when collaborating about their child's academic performance (Jong, 2011). These negative attitudes could be due to miscommunication.

The problems between the educators and the parents can stem from different communication styles (Jong 2011). Jong (2011) described two types of communication styles that conflict when educators and parents communicate about improving students' academic performance. These two conflicting communication styles are low-context communication and high-context communication (Jong, 2011). Low-context communication is the exact content that was expressed during a conversation (Jong, 2011). High-context communication depends on small cues (body language, silence or facial expression) (Jong, 2011).

Thus, the conflict occurs when one party communicates in a high contextual manner and the other party communicates in a low-contextual manner. For this reason, it is important for educators and parents to understand each other's cultural communication style to have optimal parental information for students' academic success. The diagram below provides information about characteristics of cultural context communication (Are You American? A Guide to Answering Difficult Questions Abroad, 2023).

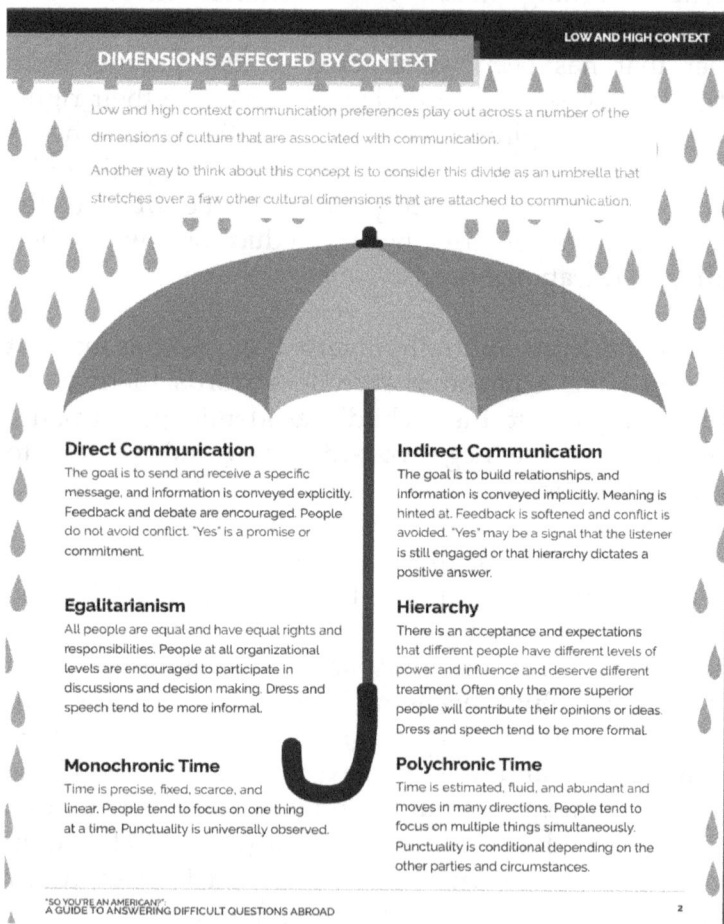

**DIMENSIONS AFFECTED BY CONTEXT**

LOW AND HIGH CONTEXT

Low and high context communication preferences play out across a number of the dimensions of culture that are associated with communication.

Another way to think about this concept is to consider this divide as an umbrella that stretches over a few other cultural dimensions that are attached to communication.

**Direct Communication**
The goal is to send and receive a specific message, and information is conveyed explicitly. Feedback and debate are encouraged. People do not avoid conflict. "Yes" is a promise or commitment.

**Indirect Communication**
The goal is to build relationships, and information is conveyed implicitly. Meaning is hinted at. Feedback is softened and conflict is avoided. "Yes" may be a signal that the listener is still engaged or that hierarchy dictates a positive answer.

**Egalitarianism**
All people are equal and have equal rights and responsibilities. People at all organizational levels are encouraged to participate in discussions and decision making. Dress and speech tend to be more informal.

**Hierarchy**
There is an acceptance and expectations that different people have different levels of power and influence and deserve different treatment. Often only the more superior people will contribute their opinions or ideas. Dress and speech tend to be more formal.

**Monochronic Time**
Time is precise, fixed, scarce, and linear. People tend to focus on one thing at a time. Punctuality is universally observed.

**Polychronic Time**
Time is estimated, fluid, and abundant and moves in many directions. People tend to focus on multiple things simultaneously. Punctuality is conditional depending on the other parties and circumstances.

"SO YOU'RE AN AMERICAN?":
A GUIDE TO ANSWERING DIFFICULT QUESTIONS ABROAD

2

*To view the completed document, check out Are You American? A Guide to Answering Difficult Questions Abroad, 2023*

## Connecting with Students from Culturally-Diverse Backgrounds

Educators can encourage academic success for students from culturally-diverse backgrounds by making a connection to their cultural learning needs (Hammond, 2015). Students from culturally-diverse backgrounds perform better in school when educators show admiration for their culture and ethnic individuality. They also are more motivated and engaged when class assignments are aligned to their culture (Irvine, 2011). Hence, educators having a multicultural fair would not only support aligning the students' cultural background to their culture, but also support an educators' interest in the students' culture.

In addition, students from multicultural backgrounds learn best in cooperative learning groups (Irvine, 2011). Educators can tap into a student's full intellectual potential by instituting cooperative learning groups for classroom instruction. For this reason, it is important for educators to understand how they can incorporate the student's culture into the instructional experience for optimal student performance.

In addition to Jong (2011) and Irvine (2011), Henderson, Mapp, and Davis (2007) discussed various ways to increase understanding of various cultural communities, and also enhance positive culture diversity. The following are the suggested approaches from Henderson, Mapp, and Davis (2007):

- Creating a team belief system that all parents from many different backgrounds and experiences goals for their children to succeed in school.
- Creating partnerships with *cultural brokers*. Henderson, Mapp, and Davis (2007) described cultural brokers as people who can guide the

school concerning families from various backgrounds. The cultural brokers are familiar with families' way of life and understand the school's culture. Moreover, the cultural brokers can provide positive strategies for faculty and parent engagement.

- Identifying and assisting with diverse parent engagement practices.
- Providing a way to support learning at home.
- Conducting meetings with people who can translate and interpret the preferred dominant language of the family.
- Maintaining professional continuous open dialogue between parents and the school faculty.

### *Sharing My Story:*

From my experience, I believe culturally diverse communication can be a two-way street for educators as well as parents. I have worked in many educationally-diverse communities. The approaches above have worked and created a more positive environment. One way I have experienced acquiring diversity information is through surveys. However, the surveys would need to be translated into different languages.

Another way I have experienced breaking the communication barrier is through the use of translators provided through my employer. I used translators for meeting and creating information letters in different languages.

Technology is a great means for communicating across different languages as well. Many devices are designed for translation purposes. I was introduced to a translator app by my niece. It was amazing the translator app provided a pathway for  both my niece and her friend to have not only a great friendship, but also great communication with one another. Moreover, my niece and her friend had different dominant languages. This is my truth that communication is the key.

## Reflective Notes

Have you ever experienced culturally diverse communication?

_____

_____

_____

How did you communicate with one another?

_____

_____

_____

How would you describe your communication style (High or low context)? Explain.

_____

_____

_____

From your experience, do you think that culturally diverse communication is a two-way street? Explain.

_____

_____

_____

# IDEA ELEVEN: PROFESSIONAL LEARNING COMMUNITY CHECKLIST

For many educators, a checklist is very helpful and a supporting guiding light. A checklist supports teachers with not only identifying the targeted task, but also exploring building capacity and sustainability measures for the learning community to flourish with fidelity. Teachers may find success with a checklist (similar to the one in Appendix B) based on the targeted professional learning community component(s) being addressed.

Roan (2022) discussed learning rounds as stakeholders using gathered targeted information to explore situations, solve problems, build capacity, and sustainability in a professional learning community. Checklists employ task-transparency among the stakeholders. The task-transparency lends itself to allowing all stakeholders to analyze, synthesize, and complete a needed component task with fidelity through discourse, even when the person who is in charge of a specific task is not present.

Also, Roan (2022) stated, "PLCs and learning rounds seek to promote a shared culture and knowledge. Both of these experiences use, analyze, and generate data around learning." Therefore, it is beneficial for professional learning community stakeholders to implement checklists not only to keep track of transparent data, but also to have a permanent product for applying the given data for learning progression. In Appendix B, an example of a checklist has been provided.

## Reflective Notes

Do you think checklists would be beneficial for your PLC's organization?

_____

_____

_____

_____

What types of items would you place on your checklist? Explain

_____

_____

_____

_____

How would you use the checklist?

_____

_____

_____

_____

# IDEA TWELVE: POSITIVE SCHOOL CLIMATE

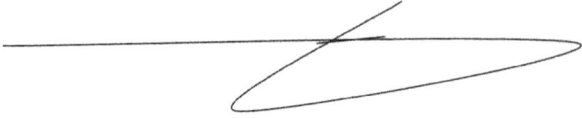

There are a variety of positive educational-organizational components that can support a healthy social and emotional school environment with outcomes of academic success. (Darling-Hammond and Paoli, 2020). An educational system with a positive school climate can positively impact a scholar's learning ability, relationships, self-esteem, and how a scholar reacts to a situation. A positive school climate can also assist educators with supporting the scholars with the above components. As a result, this will reduce stress for educators.

Moreover, staff members can utilize the positive educational organization elements for their professional pathways. However, some schools can independently employ these components, while other positive school climates components require assistance. Many positive school climate components can provide support through school teams or professional development. The positive school climate components (noted prior) are in two different categories that Darling-Hammond and Paoli (2020) discussed in the following list:

| School Climate Components that schools can institute independently | School Climate Components that schools may need supportive assistance to implement. |
|---|---|
| Advisory Systems | Stronger School-Family Connections: Providing time for teachers to meet with families. |
| Blocked School Schedules | Smaller Learning Environments |
| Interdisciplinary Teaming and Co-teaching Partnerships | Smaller Class Size |

| | |
|---|---|
| *Looping: Students stay with the same teacher for more than one school year.* | *Child Development Training* |
| *Scholars' Input Concerning Classroom Design and Management* | *Trauma and Social Identity Threat Training* |
| *Identify-Safe Environments* | *Cultural Competence Training* |
| *Social Emotional Learning* | *Social Emotional Training* |
| *Restorative Discipline Practices* | *Self- Wellness Training and Support* |

As a reminder, the chosen components are school-specific. One suggestion for schools is to meet with staff to identify which components already exist, which components are compatible with their educational system, and the components that can be utilized with ease.

## Reflective Notes

What are some positive school climate components that your educational organization can benefit from?

_____

_____

_____

_____

How can your educational organization implement the chosen positive school climate components?

_____

_____

_____

_____

# REFERENCE SECTION

American Museum of Natural History. (2023). *What is a Theory?* Retrieved from https://www.amnh.org/exhibitions/darwin/evolution-today/what-is-a-theory

Aguilar, E., & Cohen, L. (2022). *The PD Book: 7 Habits that Transform Professional Development*. Hoboken: John Wiley & Sons, INC.

Azano, A., Missett, T. C., Callahan, C. M., Oh, S., Brunner, M., Foster, L. H., & Moon, T. R. (2011). Exploring the relationship between fidelity of implementation and academic achievement in a third-grade gifted curriculum: A mixed-methods study. *Journal of Advanced Academics, 22*(5), 693–719.

Bates, B. (2016). *Learning Theories Simplified*. London: SAGE Publications Inc.

Bianco, S. D. (2010). Improving student outcomes: Data-driven instruction and fidelity of implementation in a response to intervention (RTI) model. *Teaching Exceptional Children Plus, 6*(5), 2–13.

Bouchamma, Y., & Brie, J.-M. (2014). Communities of practice and ethical leadership. *ISEA, 42*(2), 81-96.

Buffum, A., Mattos, M., & Weber, C. (2012). *Simplifying response to intervention: Four essential guiding principles*. Bloomington, IN: Solution Tree Press.

Cantrell, S. C., Almasi, J. F., Carter, J. C., & Rintamaa, M. (2013). Reading interventions in middle school and high schools: Implementation fidelity, teacher efficiency, and student achievement. *Reading Psychology, 34*, 26-58. doi:10.1080/02702711.2011.577695

Center for Comprehensive School Reform and Improvement. (2009). *Professional Learning Communities*. Retrieved from http://www.ldonline.org/article/31653#top

Century, J., Rudnick, M., & Freeman, C. (2010). A framework for measuring fidelity of implementation: A foundation for shared language and accumulation of knowledge. *American Journal of Evaluation*, 31(2), 199–218.

Coleman, M. R., Gallagher, J. J., & Job, J. (2012). Developing and sustaining professionalism within gifted education. *Gifted Child Today*, 35(1), 27–36.

Cook, B. G., & Smith, G. J. (2012). Leadership and instruction. In J. B. Crockett, B. S. Billingsley, & M. L. Boscardin, *Handbook of leadership and administration for special education* (pp. 281-269). New York, N.Y: Taylor & Francis.

Crabtree, T., Alber-Morgan, S. R., & Konrad, M. (2010). The effects of self-monitoring of story elements on reading comprehension of high school seniors with learning disabilities. *Education and Treatment of Children*, 33(2), 187-203.

Debnam, K. J., Pas, E. T., & Bradshaw, C. P. (2012). Secondary and tertiary support systems in schools implementing school-wide positive behavioral interventions and supports: A preliminary descriptive analysis. *Journal of Positive Behavior Interventions*, 14(3), 142–152.

Darling-Hammond, L., & DePaoli, J. (2020). Why school climate matters and what can be done to improve it? *National Association and State Boards of Education*, 6-48.

Retrieved from
https://nasbe.nyc3.digitaloceanspaces.com/2020/05/D
arling-Hammond-DePaoli_May-2020-Standard.pdf

FreePix. (2010-2023). Retrieved from
https://www.freepik.com/free-vector/health-doodle-
vector-happy-friendship-
concept_17224236.htm#&position=0&from_view=searc
h&track=ais&uuid=15aeba24-748c-468e-bac6-
e7db5426b5ec

Free Pix Company (2023 k). Retrieved from
https://www.freepik.com/free-photos-vectors/quill-
feather

Friend, M., Cook, L., Hurley-Chamberlain, D., &
Shamberger, C. (2010). Co-teaching: An illustration of
the complexity of collaboration in special education.
*Journal of Educational & Psychological Consultation*, 20(1),
9–27.

Fullan, M. (2007). *The new meaning of educational change* (4th
ed.). New York, NY: Teachers College Press.

Fullan, M. (2010). *All systems go: The change imperative for
whole system reform*. Thousand Oaks, CA: Corwin

Gray, J., Mitchell, R., & Tarter, J.C (2014). Organizational
and relational factors in professional learning
communities. *Planning and Changing*, v45(n), 1-2.

González, A. M. (2011). Kant's philosophy of education:
Between relational and systemic approaches. *Journal of
Philosophy of Education*, 45(3), 433–454.

Hammond, Z. (2015). *Culturally Responsive Teaching and The
Brain. Promoting Authentic Engagement and Rigor Among*

*Culturally and Linguistically Diverse Students*. London: Cowain.

Harn, B., Parisi, D., & Stoolmiller, M. (2013). Balancing Fidelity with Flexibility and Fit: What do we Really Know about Fidelity of Implementation in Schools? *Exceptional Children*, 79(2), 181-193. https://doi.org/10.1177/0014402913079002051

Harris, A., & Jones, M. (2010). Professional learning communities and system improvement. *Improving Schools*, 13(2), 172–181

Hargreaves, A., & Fullan, M. (2012). *Professional capital: Transforming teaching in every school*. New York, NY: Teachers College Press.

He, K. (2014). Learning from and thoughts of the handbook of research on educational communication and technology (3rd edition): Part-2 insights in complexity theory, situational theory, and several other hot topics. *Journal of educational technology and development*, 7(1), 1-18.

Henderson, Anne T.; Mapp, Karen L.; Johnson, Vivian R.; Davies, Don. Beyond the Bake Sale: The Essential Guide to Family/school Partnerships. The New Press. Kindle Edition.

Hirsh, S., & Hord, S. M. (2010). Building hope, giving affirmation: Learning communities that address social justice issues bring equity to the classroom. *Journal of Staff Development*, 31(4), 10–17.

Howell, R., Patton, S., & Deiotte, M. (2008). *Understanding response to intervention: A practical guide to systemic implementation*. Bloomington, IN: Solution Tree Press.

Irvine, J. J. (2012). Complex relationships between multicultural education and special education: An African American perspective. *Journal of Teacher Education*, 63(4), 268–274.

Kretlow, A. G., Cooke, N. L., & Wood, C. L. (2012). Using in-service and coaching to increase teachers' accurate use of research-based strategies. *Remedial and Special Education*, 33(6), 348–361.

Kutash, K., Cross, B., Madias, A., Duchnowski, A. J., & Green, A. L. (2012). Description of a fidelity implementation system: An example from a community-based children's mental health program. *Journal of Child and Family Studies*, 21(6), 1028–1040. https://doi.org/10.1007/s10826-012-9565-5

Lee, S., & Lang, A. (2015). Redefining Media Content and Structure in Terms of Available Resources: Toward a Dynamic Human-Centric Theory of Communication. *Communication Research*, 42(5), 599–625. https://doi.org/10.1177/0093650213488416

Mainieri, T. L., & Anderson, D. M. (2015). Exploring the black box of programing: Applying systematic implementation evaluation to a structured camp curriculum. *Journal of Experimental Education*, 38(2), 144–161. doi:10.1177/105382591424056

Mason, M. (2009). Making educational development and change sustainable: Insights from complexity theory. *International Journal of Educational Development*, 29(2), 117–124.

McLaughlin, M. J., Smith, A. F., & Wilkinson, T.G. (2012). Challenges for leaders in not so new era of standards. In J. B. Crockett, B. S. Billingsley, & M. L. Boscardin,

*Handbook of leadership and administration for special education* (pp. 361-367). New York, N.Y: Taylor & Francis.

Mertens, D. M., & Wilson, A. T. (2012). *Program evaluation theory and practice: A comprehensive guide*. New York, NY: The Guilford Press.

McIntosh, K., MacKay, L. D., Hume, A. E., Doolittle, J., Vincent, C. G., Horner, R. H., & Ervin, R. A.(2011). Development and initial validation of a measure to assess factors related to sustainability of school-wide positive behavior support. *Journal of Positive Behavior Interventions*, 13(4), 208–218.

National Research Center on Learning Disabilities. (n.d.). *Fidelity of implementation*. Retrieved October 30, 2014, from http://www.ldaofky.org/RTI/RTI%20Manual%20Secti on%204%20-%20Fidelity%20of%20Implementation.pdf

Powell, D. R., & Diamond, K. E. (2013). Implementation fidelity of a coaching-based professional development program for improving head start teachers' literacy and language instruction. *Journal of Early Intervention*, 35(2), 102-128. doi:10.1177/1053815113516678

Pugach, M. C., & Winn, Judith A. (2011). Research on co-teaching and teaming: An untapped resource for induction. *Journal of Special Education Leadership*, 24(1), 36–46.

Roan, M. (2022). *Learning Round With Teachers: Building Reflective Practitioners*. Book Design.

Reichenberg, M. (2014). The important of structure text talks for students' reading comprehension. *Journal of*

*Special Education and Rehabilitation*, 15(3-4), 77-94. doi:10.2478/JSER-2014-0012

Rosenzweig, C., Krawec, J., & Montague, M. (2011). Metacognitive strategies used of eighth-grade students with and without learning disabilities during mathematical problem solving: A think aloud analysis. *Journal of Learning Disabilities*, 44(6), 508-520. doi:10.1177/0022219410378445

RTI Action Network. (2015). *What is RTI?* Retrieved from http://www.rtinetwork.org/learn/what/whatisrti

SEDL (2014). *Professional Learning Communities What are They and Why are they Important?* Retrieved from https://sedl.org/change/issues/issues61.html

SEDL (2024). *SEDL Archive* Retrieved from https://sedl.org/about/

Skalski, A. K., & Romero, M. (2011). Data-based decision making. *Principal Leadership*, 11(5), 12–16. Retrieved from http://www.nasponline.org/resources/principals/Data_Use_Jan11_NASSP.PDF

So You Are American? A Guide to Answering Difficult Questions Aboard. (2023). Retrieved from https://www.state.gov/courses/answeringdifficultquestions/assets/m/resources/DifficultQuestions-LowandHighContext.pdf

Sulkowski, M. L., Wingfield, R. J., Jones, D., & Coulter, W. A. (2011). Response to intervention and interdisciplinary collaboration: Joining hands to support children's healthy development. *Journal of Applied School Psychology*, 27(2), 118–133.

The University of the State of New York & The State Education Department. (2010). *Response to intervention: Guidance for New York state school districts.* Retrieved from http://www.p12.nysed.gov/specialed/RTI/guidance-oct10.pdf.

U.S. Department of Education. (2003). *Identifying and implementing educational practices supported by rigorous evidence: A user friendly guide.* Retrieved from http://www2.ed.gov/rschstat/research/pubs/rigorousevid/index.html

Waldron, N. L., & McLeskey, J. (2010). Establishing a collaborative school culture through comprehensive school reform. *Journal of Educational and Psychological Consultation, 20*(1), 58–74.

Wart, M. V. (2013). Lessons from leadership theory and the contemporary challenges of leaders. *Public Administration Review,* 553-565.

Wilcox, K.C & Angelis, J.I (2012). From "muddle school" to middle school: Building capacity to collaborate for higher-performing middle schools: High-performing level schools build capacity to support collaboration and student success. *Middle School Journal, 43*(4);40-48

Zepada, S. J., Parylo, O., & Bengtson, E. (2014). Analyzing principal's professional development practices through the lens of adult learning theory. *Professional Development in Education, 40*(2), 295-315.

# APPENDIX SECTION

# APPENDIX A: REFLECTIVE NOTES

Reflective Notes

What resonated with you the most? Explain.

_____

_____

_____

Did you make any connections (self, real-world or other text)? Explain.

_____

_____

_____

How would you apply what resonated with you the most?

_____

_____

_____

# APPENDIX B: PROFESSIONAL LEARNING COMMUNITY CHECKLIST

## *Professional Learning Community Checklist Example*

Grade/Subject:

Topic:

Team(s):

Data Driven Instruction:

Educational Policy that guides educational practice:

Attendees:

|  | Time | Meeting place | Funding | Outcome |
|---|---|---|---|---|
| A needs assessment evaluation |  |  |  |  |
| A building capacity evaluation |  |  |  |  |
| Replication/Transportability Exportability Evaluation |  |  |  |  |
| Monitoring Evaluation |  |  |  |  |
| Developmental Evaluation |  |  |  |  |
| Implementation Evaluation |  |  |  |  |
| Sustainability Evaluation |  |  |  |  |
| Collaboration |  |  |  |  |
| Debriefing |  |  |  |  |

Additional Notes

# APPENDIX B: PROFESSIONAL LEARNING COMMUNITY SLIDES

PROFESSIONAL LEARNING COMMUNITIES AND PROFESSIONAL INFRASTRUCTURES

BY: DR. NATASHA COX-MAGNO

# GUIDING QUESTIONS

- What are professional learning communities (PLC)?
- Who are the people involved in professional learning communities (PLC)?
- What are the characteristics of professional learning communities (PLC)?
- What are professional infrastructures that support Professional learning communities (PLC) ?
- How are Professional infrastructures aligned to Professional learning communities (PLC) ?
- How does educational policies guide professional practices in Professional learning communities(PLC)?

## EDUCATIONAL POLICIES THAT GUIDE PROFESSIONAL PRACTICES FOR PLC

○ 2001 Reauthorization of ESEA required the following from the states:

- Rigorous academics and achievement standards.
- Measure students' state assessment peformance to state standards.
  - Districts and Schools are accountable for meeting pre-specific levels of students' performance on assessments, attendance and graduation rates.
  - Accountability is based on aggregate students' performance and disaggregate students' performance.
    - Included subgroups and students with disabilities.

(McLaughlin, Smith & Wilkinson, 2012)

# PROFESSIONAL INFRASTRUCTURES THAT SUPPORT PLC:

- Professional infrastructures :
  - Provide a time for educators to collaborate.
  - Provide a place for educators to collaborate.
  - Ensure that resources are available for educators.
  - Participate in the collaborative data driven decision-making process.
  - Provide collaboration across schools
  - Provide rules to ensure that all educators are involve in the collaborative process.
  - Provide on-going professional developments to sustain continuous improvement of educators' knowledge
  - Provide coaching support to assist educators that did not fully comprehend a previous professional development.

(Coleman, Gallagher, and Job, 2012 ;Hirsh & Hord, 2010; Buffum, Mattos, & Weber, 2012; Hargreaves & Fullan, 2012)

## DEFINING PROFESSIONAL LEARNING COMMUNITIES

- Professional learning communities (PLC) is an organizational system implemented to assist educators in increasing their knowledge to sustain continuously students' learning performance using collaboration.

(The Center for Continuous Reform, 2009; Hargreaves & Fullan, 2012; The Center for Continuous Reform, 2009).

## SCHOOL PERSONAL INVOLVED IN PLC

- Administrators
- General Education Teachers
- Special Education Teachers
- English Language Learner Teachers
- Resource Room Teachers
- Cluster Teachers
- Paraprofessionals
- Related Service Providers
- School Nurses

## PLC'S CHARACTERISTICS

- A shared vision
- A collaborative culture
- Focus on improving students' learning performance
- Supportive environment
- Shared leadership
- Shared personal practices
- Collective Responsibility
- Professional development

(The Center for Continuous Reform, 2009 ; Harris & Jones, 2010; SEDL Advance Research Improving Education, 2014)

CREATING A PROFESSIONAL LEARNING COMMUNITIES AT WORK: FOUNDATIONAL CONCEPTS AND PRACTICES

https://www.youtube.com/watch?v=FLGHY9-sibA&t=3s

# SOLUTION TREE: RICK DUFOUR ON THE IMPORTANCE OF PLC

https://www.youtube.com/watch?v=MnWDJFxfAKE&t=1s

www.ingramcontent.com/pod-product-compliance
Lightning Source LLC
Chambersburg PA
CBHW060240030426
42335CB00014B/1551